Facts About the North American Porcupine

By Lisa Strattin

© 2016 Lisa Strattin

Revised © 2022 Lisa Strattin

FREE BOOK

FREE FOR ALL SUBSCRIBERS

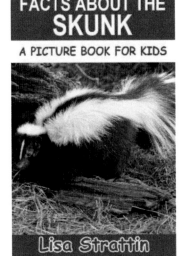

LisaStrattin.com/Subscribe-Here

BOX SET

- **FACTS ABOUT THE POISON DART FROGS**
- **FACTS ABOUT THE THREE TOED SLOTH**
  - **FACTS ABOUT THE RED PANDA**
  - **FACTS ABOUT THE SEAHORSE**
  - **FACTS ABOUT THE PLATYPUS**
  - **FACTS ABOUT THE REINDEER**
  - **FACTS ABOUT THE PANTHER**
- **FACTS ABOUT THE SIBERIAN HUSKY**

LisaStrattin.com/BookBundle

Facts for Kids Picture Books by Lisa Strattin

Little Blue Penguin, Vol 92

Chipmunk, Vol 5

Frilled Lizard, Vol 39

Blue and Gold Macaw, Vol 13

Poison Dart Frogs, Vol 50

Blue Tarantula, Vol 115

African Elephants, Vol 8

Amur Leopard, Vol 89

Sabre Tooth Tiger, Vol 167

Baboon, Vol 174

Sign Up for New Release Emails Here

LisaStrattin.com/subscribe-here

★★COVER IMAGE★★

https://www.flickr.com/photos/usfwspacific/51817322337/

★★ADDITIONAL IMAGES★★

https://www.flickr.com/photos/fsnorthernregion/52098618288/

https://www.flickr.com/photos/jschauma/4626896281/

https://www.flickr.com/photos/seamus_walsh/214998749/

https://www.flickr.com/photos/pelican/19330426/

https://www.flickr.com/photos/144871758@N05/49274685136/

https://www.flickr.com/photos/usfwsnortheast/7152279461/

https://www.flickr.com/photos/douglas_mcgrady/34583594696/

https://www.flickr.com/photos/79666107@N00/6299991648/

https://www.flickr.com/photos/usfwsmtnprairie/52259088748

https://www.flickr.com/photos/15016964@N02/4671834858/

Contents

INTRODUCTION

North American Porcupines are small- to medium-sized animals. They live in the United States and Canada. They like to climb trees and have sharp needle-like projections protruding from their bodies. They live in a wide range of habitats. Their behaviors vary on where they live. They can tolerate colder temperatures than any other porcupine species.

These porcupines are solitary animals. They only come together to raise a family and to mate. They use chemical scents to mark territories and indicate mating status. North American Porcupines are herbivorous and eat a large variety of plants. They avoid predation by climbing up trees or rolling into balls.

CHARACTERISTICS

North American Porcupines are not social creatures and usually live alone; however, they will sometimes share dens in the winter. They can also be seen in groups when foraging for food during the winter.

They defend their territories from other porcupines. They usually don't leave their territory unless food is very scarce. When an invader enters a porcupine's territory, they will chatter their teeth and show black and white markings on their tails. This tells the intruder to leave or get ready to fight.

They can communicate vocally with high-pitched screeches. Unlike other animals, female porcupines move away, and males will stay.

North American Porcupines have a very unique defense mechanism they use to avoid enemies. They are covered with long sharp quills or needles. They flash these quills to warn enemies to stay away. If the enemies do not leave, the porcupine can stick their enemies with these needles. The quills have hooks on the sides that make them very painful and difficult to remove. Each porcupine has around 30,000 quills!

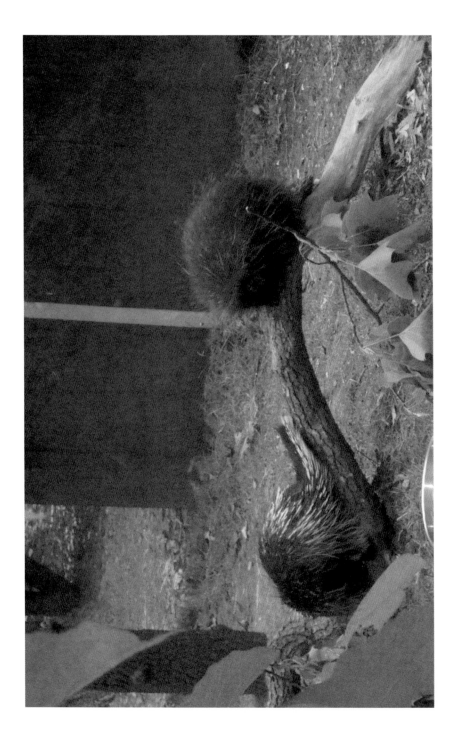

APPEARANCE

North American Porcupines are the second largest rodent in North American after the North American beaver. They have a stocky form, and they waddle when they walk. The quills cover their head, legs, back, and tail and are colored with bright white tips to warn enemies to stay away.

North American Porcupines do not have canine teeth. They are dark brown to black in color and have a black stripe on their lower back and in the center of their tail.

LIFE STAGES

The first life stage for the North American Porcupine is the juvenile life stage. This begins when a female porcupine gives birth to one or two juvenile porcupines after mating. The mating period occurs during October and November, with pregnancy lasting from 205 to 217 days. This means that porcupines are born in the springtime.

Juveniles will nurse from their mother until they are around three months old. Female juveniles stay with their mothers for about five months while males stay up to one year. Females become adults before the males. Females enter the adult life stage in 22 to 25 months and males become adults in 29 months.

The adult stage is the final life stage.

LIFE SPAN

North American Porcupines can live up to 18 years in the wild if they are in a suitable habitat. However, the average lifespan is six years. There is not any information available, as of this writing, regarding how long they can live in captivity.

SIZE

North American Porcupines are the second largest rodent in North American after the North American beaver. They are considered a small to medium-sized animal.

Adult males weigh an average of 22 to 27 pounds and the adult females weigh between 15 to 18 pounds.

HABITAT

North American Porcupines can live in a wide range of habitats. They live in deciduous forests in the eastern United States and Canada to the semi-arid dry regions in the southwestern United States. They are also able to live at a high range of elevation.

North American Porcupines adapt their behavior to their home environment. In New York, USA, porcupines spend most of their time climbing in trees. However, in locations without tall trees, they will spend more time on the ground.

DIET

North American Porcupines eat only plants. However, they eat a wide variety of plants that differs throughout the year, depending on the plant's chemistry. In the summer they will focus on feeding on high protein foods and spend very little time eating. However, in the fall and winter when food becomes scarce, they spend a considerable amount of time feeding.

In the southwestern United States, they will feed on the bark and needles of Pinyon Pine and Ponderosa Pine trees. In the northeastern United States, they will feed on leaves of Maple and Beech trees. Their diet can vary considerably throughout the year, and during the winter they will feed on more twigs and bark because other food sources are scarce. They will also feed on the salt left over that has been applied to cars to melt snow.

FRIENDS AND ENEMIES

North American Porcupines are not very social animals and do not have many friends. They are only friendly with other porcupines during the mating season and when females are raising juveniles. They will interact with other porcupines through vocal calls and scent markings.

They have several enemies. Bobcats, coyotes, wolves, cougars, mink, lynx, wolverines, and owls are all enemies of these porcupines. They will attack porcupines of all life stages. Porcupines use their sharp quills as a defense mechanism against being attacked; however, this is not always successful.

People can be enemies of porcupines. People consider porcupines as pests and will try to get rid of them.

SUITABILITY AS PETS

North American Porcupines would likely not be suitable pets. Although, you are allowed to keep them as pets in several states with the proper permits. They do have very unique food requirements that can make it difficult to find the proper feed for them. Their diets require foods are high in nitrogen and salt.

Their defense of quills can be very painful, so you should probably look for a more suitable and huggable pet instead of the North American Porcupine.

COLOR ME

COLOR ME

COLOR ME

COLOR ME

COLOR ME

COLOR ME

COLOR ME

COLOR ME

COLOR ME

COLOR ME

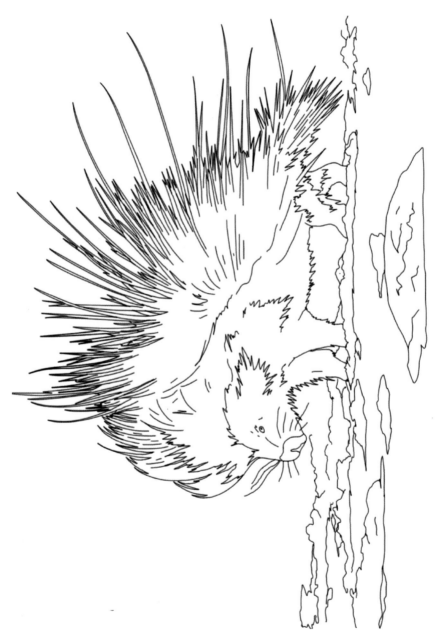

Please leave me a review here:

LisaStrattin.com/Review-Vol-120

For more Kindle Downloads Visit Lisa Strattin Author Page on Amazon Author Central

amazon.com/author/lisastrattin

To see upcoming titles, visit my website at LisaStrattin.com– most books available on Kindle!

LisaStrattin.com

FREE BOOK

FOR ALL SUBSCRIBERS – SIGN UP NOW

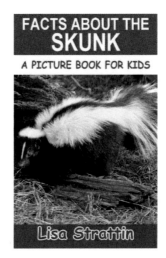

LisaStrattin.com/Subscribe-Here

LisaStrattin.com/Facebook

LisaStrattin.com/Youtube

Made in the USA
Middletown, DE
05 October 2022

12011065R00024